NATURE'S
CHILDREN™

CAMELS

by Jennifer Zeiger

Children's Press®

An Imprint of Scholastic Inc.
New York Toronto London Auckland Sydney
Mexico City New Delhi Hong Kong
Danbury, Connecticut

Content Consultant
Dr. Stephen S. Ditchkoff
Professor of Wildlife Sciences
Auburn University
Auburn, Alabama

Photographs ©: Alamy Images: 18, 19 (TGB), 28 (Wildlife GmbH);
Dreamstime: 2 background, 3 background, 44 background, 45
background (Roy Mattappallil Thomas); Getty Images: 1, 8 (Danita
Delimont), 5 bottom, 38, 39 (Fayez Nureldine); Media Bakery/
Bernard: 20, 21; Reuters: 40, 41; Science Source: 16, 17 (Cheryl
Power), 32, 33 (Krystyna Szulecka), 26, 27 (Phil Degginger);
Shutterstock, Inc.: 5 top, 10, 11 (simoly), 30, 31 (Zazaa Mongolia);
Superstock, Inc.: 6, 7 (Dave Stamboulis), 4, 5 background, 22, 22
(Exotica), 35 (Steve Bloom Images); Thinkstock: 2, 3, 14,15, 24, 25,
46 (Guenter Guni), cover (mrandrewmurray), 36 (Ruediger Meier),
12 (Sergejs Razvodovskis).

Library of Congress Cataloging-in-Publication Data
Zeiger, Jennifer, author.
  Camels / by Jennifer Zeiger.
    pages cm. — (Nature's children)
  Summary: "This book details the life and habits of camels."—
Provided by publisher.
  Audience: Ages 9–12.
  Audience: Grades 4 to 6.
  Includes bibliographical references and index.
  ISBN 978-0-531-21170-0 (library binding : alk. paper) —
  ISBN 978-0-531-21189-2 (pbk. : alk. paper)
  1. Camels–Juvenile literature. I. Title. II. Series: Nature's children
(New York, N.Y.)
  QL737.U54Z45 2015
  599.63'62–dc23   2014029884

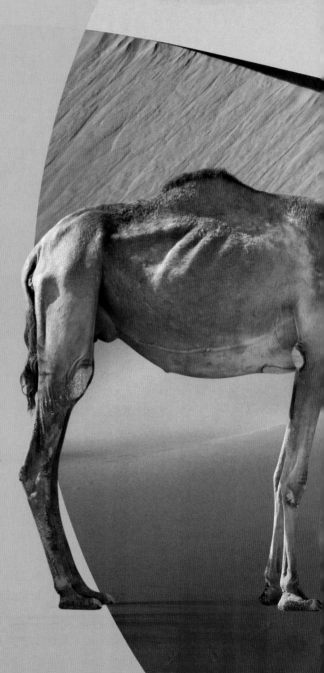

All rights reserved. Published in 2015 by Children's Press, an imprint
of Scholastic Inc.

Printed in China 62
SCHOLASTIC, CHILDREN'S PRESS, and associated logos are
trademarks and/or registered trademarks of Scholastic Inc.

1 2 3 4 5 6 7 8 9 10 R 24 23 22 21 20 19 18 17 16 15

Camels

Class	Mammalia
Order	Cetartiodactyla
Family	Camelidae
Genus	*Camelus*
Species	Two species (*Camelus dromedarius* and *Camelus bactrianus*)
World distribution	Domestic dromedaries live across northern Africa into southwestern Asia; a small population of feral dromedaries lives in Australia; domestic Bactrian camels live in the Middle East, Mongolia, and China; wild Bactrian camels live in China and Mongolia, particularly the Gobi desert
Habitats	Most live in deserts; some live in grasslands or steppe regions
Distinctive physical characteristics	One or two humps located on its back; long neck and narrow head; short tail; thin legs and wide feet; large eyes protected by thick eyebrows and eyelashes; fur ranging from light, sandy brown or gray to dark brown; Bactrian camels have thicker fur than dromedaries, especially in winter
Habits	Most camels are domesticated for use as pack animals or raised for their fur, milk, and meat; wild Bactrian camels live in herds and move as necessary in search of food and water, staying near water sources in winter and traveling farther in spring and summer
Diet	Herbivorous; mainly eat grasses, shrubs, and other plants

CAMELS

Contents

CHAPTER 1

Out of the Desert

Deep in the Gobi desert, it is a windy day. Bits of dirt and dust fill the air. Not far off, a spring feeds a small **oasis**. A herd of six or seven unusual creatures can be seen plodding steadily toward the water source. The two humps on each of their backs sag to the side. They are wild Bactrian camels, and they are visiting the oasis to refresh themselves. After weeks in the desert, they fill themselves with fresh water and juicy plants.

The camels soon move on. As they digest the food and water they have consumed, their humps become a little fuller. The herd journeys on into the **arid**, empty landscape. They are confident of finding some dry grasses or short, thorny plants that other animals have overlooked or did not want.

Food and water are often rare in camels' natural homes.

One Hump or Two?

There are two **species** of camel: Bactrian and dromedary. Bactrians are divided into **domestic** and wild subspecies. Bactrian camels have two humps. All dromedaries are domestic and have only one hump.

All camels are covered in brown or gray fur, but Bactrian fur tends to be darker and thicker. A Bactrian's coat becomes even thicker during winter so it can survive the frigid temperatures. Both types have long necks, narrow heads, and short tails. A camel's four slender legs end in wide feet. Each foot has two toes that are fused together. Camels walk by stepping with both left feet at the same time, then both right feet.

Camels can grow to reach heights of more than 7 feet (2 meters) at the top of their humps. A male dromedary might weigh 1,600 pounds (726 kilograms). A male Bactrian camel weighs a little more. Female camels of either type tend to be slightly smaller.

Adult male
6 ft. (1.8 m)

Camel
7 ft. (2 m) tall

A dromedary's single hump sets it apart from its Bactrian cousins.

CHAPTER 2

Masters of Survival

Camels are famous for their ability to survive in some of the world's harshest habitats. They are most often found in places where water is scarce and temperatures are extreme. For example, temperatures can reach above 130 degrees Fahrenheit (54 degrees Celsius) in the African Sahara. Fewer than 10 inches (25 centimeters) of rain generally fall there in a year. The desert that covers much of the Arabian Peninsula has a similar climate. In Mongolia, China, and other areas where Bactrian camels are found, the deserts and steppes are often just as dry, but cooler. Summer temperatures may rise above 100°F (38°C), but they plummet in winter. In the Gobi desert, temperatures may drop to –20°F (–29°C) or lower.

In such climates, the ground is generally dry and often rocky or sandy. Outside of the occasional oasis, it is difficult for plants to grow. This makes it difficult for many animals to find food. However, camels have ways of surviving.

Camels are able to survive in a variety of harsh conditions.

Saving Up for Later

A camel's humps are not just for looks. They actually play an important role in allowing a camel to survive for long periods of time with little food or water. Humps are made up of energy-rich fat. A camel stores up this fat when food and water are easily available. During these times, camels eat and drink as much as they can. Sometimes they even overeat. Their humps become tall and full.

When food or water is scarce, camels use the nutrients in their humps to survive. Over time, the humps start to sag as the fat disappears. In a severe shortage, a camel's humps may disappear altogether. Camels can live up to a week with no water at all. If camels can find water but no food, they might live for months. Camels have been known to live up to a year with limited resources.

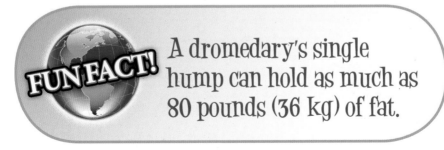

FUN FACT! A dromedary's single hump can hold as much as 80 pounds (36 kg) of fat.

A camel's humps begin to sag over as it uses up the nutrients inside.

Losing and Gaining

Like other mammals, camels are warm-blooded. Their bodies naturally produce heat. Because camels spend most of their time in high temperatures, they must get rid of this heat as fast as possible. Fat is an insulator. Animals in cold climates often store a layer of fat all over their bodies to keep them warm. A camel keeps most of its fat in its humps. This allows heat to escape quickly from the rest of its body.

Camels lose body heat quickly, but they must lose moisture as slowly as possible. If camels sweated as much as humans, they would not last long in the desert. Camels start sweating when temperatures reach above 106°F (41°C). Even then, they sweat very little. Camels also replenish their water supplies very quickly. A camel can drink 25 gallons (95 liters) of water in 10 minutes. Other animals could die trying to drink so much so fast.

FUN FACT! Wild Bactrian camels, unlike most mammals and even other camels, can drink salt water when nothing else is available.

Camels drink water wherever they can find it.

Feet and Face

A camel's head and feet are just as remarkable as its humps. The feet are wide and expand when pressed against the ground. This provides a secure footing against soft sand and other surfaces. Pads on the bottom of the feet act as tough but flexible armor. They protect the feet from hot sand, sharp rocks, and other possible hazards.

In dry climates, winds carry sand, soil, and other particles into the air. A camel's long, double row of eyelashes helps keep these particles out of its eyes. Each eye is also protected by a special **membrane** that keeps particles out but allows light in so the camel can see. Camels can close their large nostrils to keep particles from blowing into their noses, too.

Take a close look at a camel's mouth. Its top lip is actually separated into two parts. Each of these parts can move independently. This allows the camel to grip the often short, dry, thorny plants it eats and rip them out of the ground.

A camel's flexible face gives it precise control over its lips and nostrils.

CHAPTER 3

From Desert to Steppe

Camels are perhaps most often associated with the wide, sweeping deserts of northern Africa. This is at least partially true of dromedary camels. They are mainly found in Sudan and Somalia, as well as in the Middle East. Some live as far east as southwestern Asia, into India. There is also a feral population in Australia's desert outback region. Most dromedaries are domesticated, bred by humans over thousands of years.

Bactrian camels are most often found to the north and east of the dromedaries. Domesticated Bactrians live across parts of the Middle East and into China and Mongolia in southeastern Asia in deserts and steppe regions. A very small population of wild Bactrian camels lives in China and Mongolia. These camels are almost exclusively found in and around the Gobi desert.

Feral dromedaries are found only in the wild outback of Australia.

Dinnertime

Camels are herbivores. Near a major source of water, a camel can easily find juicy leaves and grasses. Farther into the desert, the grasses, shrubs, and other plants tend to be shorter and tougher. Many have defenses, such as thorns, to discourage animals from eating them. Thanks to their muscular lips, camels have no trouble eating these tough plants.

Camels, like cows and certain other mammals, are ruminants. This means they chew and swallow their food more than once. A camel's stomach has three chambers, or parts. When food is first chewed and swallowed, it goes into the first two chambers. There, the food softens, then is regurgitated into the camel's mouth as cud. The camel chews the cud, breaking the plant matter down further, making digestion easier. When the camel swallows again, the food returns to the stomach, where digestion continues.

FUN FACT! Camels sometimes spit when they are excited or angry. This spit is a mix of saliva and stomach contents.

Camels can eat even the toughest, driest plants.

Life in the Herd

Nearly all the world's camels are domestic and are cared for by humans. In the wild, camels live in herds. Wild Bactrians usually form herds of around 6 to 20 camels. Most herds include one dominant male, several females, and their young. Some male camels are not attached to a group of females. Several young males will often join together to form a herd with no females. Others live on their own.

Wild herds **migrate** as the seasons change. In winter, herds stay near a water source where food will be easier to find. As summer comes and temperatures rise, food becomes more plentiful. The camels can move off into more arid regions.

Members of a herd have many ways to communicate with one another. This includes anything from a quiet moan or high-pitched bleat to a loud bellow or roar. Mothers and their **calves** often hum to each other to give comfort and show affection.

Traveling in herds provides camels with safety and companionship.

Camel Calves

Camels **mate** during the wettest time of year, around January or February. During this time, male camels make special bellowing calls to attract females. They also fight other males for control of herds. A herd's dominant male is the only male to mate with the herd's adult females.

After mating, a female camel is pregnant for just over a year. Around March or April, she finds a private place to give birth, normally to a single calf. A newborn calf usually weighs about 80 pounds (36 kg). It is able to walk soon after it is born. It looks much like a smaller version of an adult camel. It has no humps yet, but there are tufts of thick fur on its back where its humps will eventually grow.

Mother and calf spend two weeks on their own before joining the rest of the herd. A calf drinks its mother's milk for about a year, then moves to a diet of plants. After three or four years, a young camel is ready to have calves of its own. Young males must leave their mother's herd to find their own herd.

Mother camels form close bonds with their calves.

CHAPTER 4

A Long History

Camels are part of the family Camelidae. Some 40 million years ago, the first camelids lived in North America. Some of the earliest species were much smaller than today's camels. Researchers have found fossils of camelids that were about the size of rabbits. They roamed across North America's mountains, grasslands, and deserts.

About three million years ago, shallower oceans left a strip of land called the Bering Land Bridge exposed between modern-day Alaska and Russia. Around this time, a group of camelids migrated across this land bridge into Asia. Over the centuries, the animals moved south and farther west. They settled across parts of Asia and the Middle East, extending into eastern Europe and south into Africa. Camels eventually disappeared from North America and Europe. However, they were introduced elsewhere by humans, including southern Asia and the most arid regions of northern Africa. In the 1800s, camels were even brought as far as Australia. This population was left to grow feral outside of human control.

Though this ancient camelid species no longer exists, its fossilized skeleton offers valuable information about the way it lived.

Family Relations

The two species of camels we know today are called *dromedarius*, or dromedary, and *bactrianus*, or Bactrian. Almost all of the world's camels are domesticated. The wild Bactrian subspecies makes up a tiny fraction of the camel population. There are only about 1,000 wild Bactrians living today.

Scientists have debated about how these species of camels are related to each other. Many argued that all of today's domesticated dromedaries and Bactrians were just variations of wild Bactrians that had been bred by humans. However, recent research has shown that the two species are actually quite different from each other. They likely developed independently millions of years ago.

FUN FACT! Roughly 90 percent of the world's camels are dromedaries.

Because they are mostly domesticated, camels are commonly seen alongside people.

A Special Relationship

For thousands of years, domesticated camels have had a very close relationship with humans. Bactrian camels were first domesticated as much as 4,500 years ago. The once-wild dromedaries were domesticated some 500 years later. Ever since, camels have been incredibly important to people, especially camel herders and nomadic groups such as the Bedouin.

People keep camels for their wool, meat, and milk. They also collect camel dung, which is used as fuel for fires. In addition, camels are an excellent mode of transportation. They can run up to 40 miles (65 kilometers) per hour for short distances. They can also plod along slowly for many miles a day. Camels are strong and often used as pack animals. Bactrian camels can carry a load of 440 pounds (200 kg) across 30 miles (48 km) in a single day. Dromedaries can carry about half that over similar distances.

Camels can carry heavy burdens with little difficulty.

Wild Relatives

As camels migrated north and crossed the Bering Land Bridge into Asia, another group of camelids moved south. These animals developed into today's guanacos, vicuñas, llamas, and alpacas of South America.

Guanacos and vicuñas are wild. Guanacos live along the Andes Mountains from Peru and Bolivia, south into the islands at the tip of South America. Vicuñas are mostly found in Peru, Bolivia, and parts of Chile and Argentina. Unlike camels, guanacos and vicuñas have no humps on their backs. Their fur coat is also thicker than a camel's. However, they do have the same long legs and neck as the rest of the camelid family, as well as wide, padded feet. The climate is dry in much of their habitat, so they get nearly all of the water they need from the plants they eat. Like wild Bactrian camels, guanacos and vicuñas usually live in herds with several females and a male, in all-male herds, or as independent males.

Guanacos have brown fur on their backs and white undersides.

Domestic Relatives

Llamas and alpacas are both domesticated. Most experts agree they were domesticated from wild guanacos thousands of years ago. Llamas and alpacas are used most often as pack animals but also for their wool, meat, and dung.

Llamas are found across Bolivia, Peru, Ecuador, Chile, and Argentina. They are especially common in and around the Andes Mountains. Alpacas mostly live in the mountains of Bolivia and Peru. There is little oxygen high in the mountains where these animals live. Extra red blood cells in their blood hold more oxygen, which allows them to survive. Llamas and alpacas have long, thick coats of fur that keep them warm in their colder habitat. They do not have humps like camels. However, they do have long legs and necks like their relatives. Llamas can also survive several days without water, similar to camels.

Alpacas are often raised for their thick, warm fur, which is used to make yarn.

CHAPTER 5

Humans and Camels

Camels help people in many ways, but they have also caused problems. In the 1800s, people brought dromedaries to Australia for transportation and other work. The camels were useful at first. However, cars and other motorized vehicles became popular in the early 20th century. After that, the camels were no longer needed. Most were set free.

The dromedaries thrived on their own in the dry Australian outback. Today, their presence wreaks havoc on the local ecosystem. Feral camels drink a lot of the available water. They also eat so much vegetation that some plants have nearly gone extinct. There is little food left for other herbivores. Also, herds of camels have destroyed buildings, water lines, and fences. Camels are sometimes hit by vehicles. This can also injure or kill drivers and passengers. Organizations are working to reduce Australia's camel population and find ways to make the animals useful rather than destructive.

Automobiles can pose a major threat to camels living in areas where there are many people.

Outbreak

In more recent years, camels have been linked to a new illness called Middle East respiratory syndrome (MERS). Though related to the common cold, the MERS virus is more severe. It can cause fever, coughing, organ failure, and even death in some cases.

As the name indicates, MERS first appeared in the Middle East. The first known infections in humans were in Saudi Arabia in 2012. The virus soon spread into surrounding countries, parts of Europe, and the United States. Hundreds of people became infected. About one-third of them died.

By 2014, many experts believed that the virus came from camels. Governments of affected countries warned people to wear masks and gloves around camels. They also warned people to wash their hands, thoroughly cook camel meat, and boil camel milk. Such actions have helped cut down on the number of infections, but new cases still occur. Researchers are still figuring out how best to treat the virus and prevent it from spreading.

Masks can help protect people who work with camels from being infected with MERS.

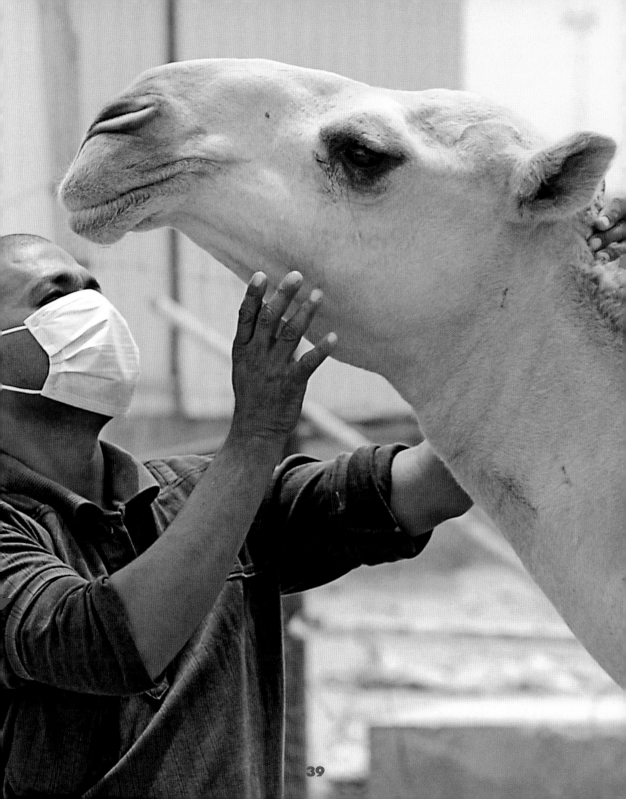

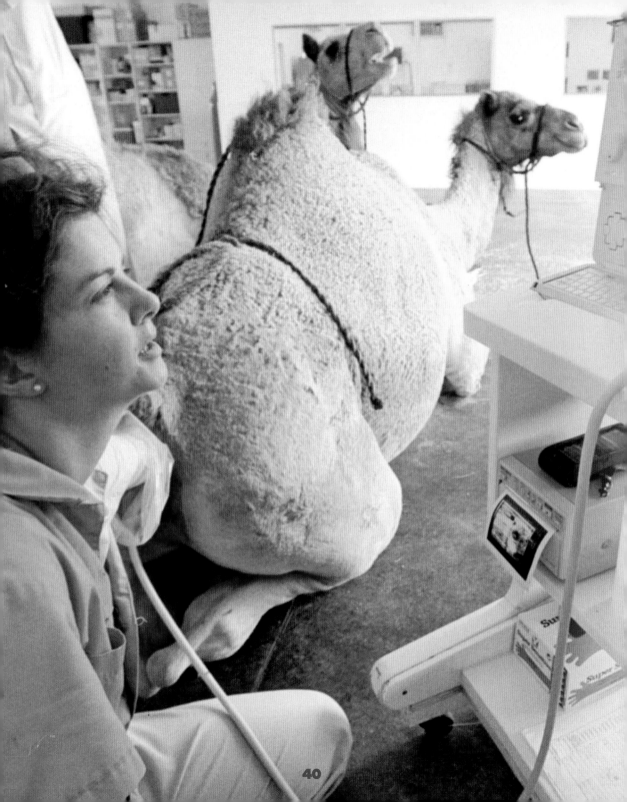

Losing Camels

Humans also cause serious problems for camels. Today, wild Bactrian camels are critically **endangered**. There are fewer than 1,000 living in the wild. In 50 years, the population may fall by 80 percent. Humans and wolves hunt them. The camels compete with domestic camels and other **livestock** for food and water. They also compete with humans for space. Mining projects, ranches, homes, businesses, and other human activities are taking up more and more space. As a result, many wild camels struggle to find food and water. They do not always have the space to migrate. Special reserves have been created in China and Mongolia to protect some wild Bactrian territory. There is also a growing effort to help breed these camels and increase the population. Scientists are studying how effective these actions are.

Humans have a complicated relationship with camels. Some parts are good, others are not. But no matter what, camels are an important part of this world, and that will likely not change.

A veterinarian monitors the process of a camel's pregnancy using an ultrasound device.

Words to Know

arid (AIR-id) — extremely dry because of a lack of rain

calves (CAVZ) — the young of several large species of animals, including camels

cud (KUHD) — regurgitated food that a ruminant chews and swallows again

domestic (duh-MES-tik) — animals that have been tamed; people use them as a source of food or as work animals, or keep them as pets

ecosystem (EE-koh-sis-tuhm) — all the living things in a place and their relation to the environment

endangered (en-DAYN-jurd) — at risk of becoming extinct, usually because of human activity

extinct (ik-STINGKT) — no longer found alive; known about only through fossils or history

family (FAM-uh-lee) — a group of living things that are related to each other

feral (FARE-uhl) — formerly captive and currently living in the wild

fossils (FAH-suhlz) — bones, shells, or other traces of an animal or plant from millions of years ago, preserved as rock

herbivores (HUR-buh-vorz) — animals that only eat plants

insulator (IN-suh-lay-tur) — a material that prevents heat from escaping

livestock (LIVE-stahk) — animals that are kept or raised on a farm or ranch, often being allowed to roam freely

mammals (MAM-uhlz) — warm-blooded animals that have hair or fur and usually give birth to live babies; female mammals produce milk to feed their young

mate (MAYT) — to join together to produce babies

membrane (MEM-brane) — a very thin layer of tissue that lines or covers certain organs or cells

migrate (MYE-grate) — to move to another area or climate at a particular time of year

nomadic (noh-MAD-ik) — lacking a fixed home; nomadic animals or people move from place to place as necessary

oasis (oh-AY-sis) — a place in a desert where water can be found above the ground and where plants and trees can grow

regurgitated (ri-GUR-ji-tay-tid) — brought food from the stomach back up to the mouth

respiratory (RES-pur-uh-tor-ee) — having to do with an animal's ability to breathe

ruminants (ROO-muh-nuhnts) — cud-chewing, hoofed mammals that have a stomach divided into three or four chambers

species (SPEE-sheez) — one of the groups into which animals and plants of the same genus are divided; members of the same species can mate and have offspring

steppes (STEPS) — the wide, treeless plains found in southeastern Europe and Asia

virus (VYE-ruhs) — a very tiny organism that can reproduce and grow only when inside living cells; viruses cause diseases such as polio, measles, the common cold, and AIDS

Habitat Map

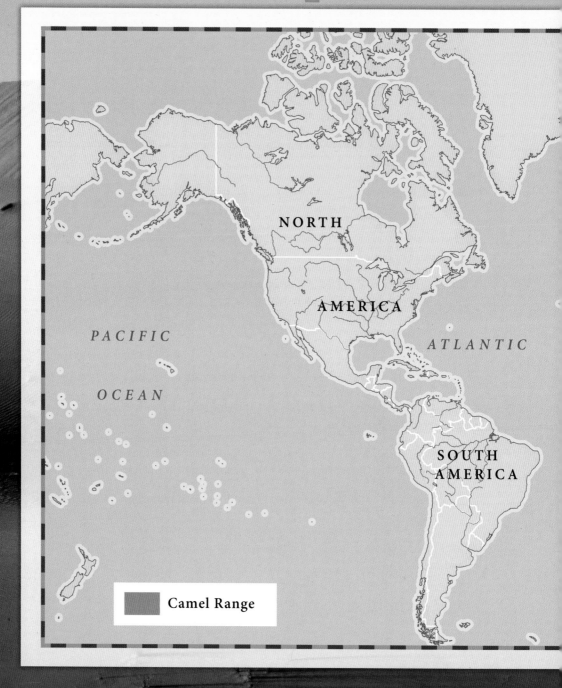

NORTH

AMERICA

PACIFIC

OCEAN

ATLANTIC

SOUTH
AMERICA

Camel Range

ARCTIC OCEAN

EUROPE

ASIA

AFRICA

PACIFIC
OCEAN

INDIAN

OCEAN

OCEAN

AUSTRALIA

Find Out More

Books

Borgert-Spaniol, Megan. *Camels*. Minneapolis: Bellwether Media, 2012.

Gish, Melissa. *Camels*. Mankato, MN: Creative Paperbacks, 2013.

Gray, Susan Heinrichs. *Camels Have Humps*. Ann Arbor, MI: Cherry Lake Publishing, 2015.

Visit this Scholastic Web site for more information on camels:
www.factsfornow.scholastic.com
Enter the keyword **Camels**

Index

Page numbers in *italics* indicate a photograph or map.

About the Author

Jennifer Zeiger lives in Chicago, Illinois, where she writes and edits books for children.